Silencing Satan

Silencing Satan

Handbook of Biblical Demonology
13 Studies for Individuals and Groups

SHARON BEEKMANN

WIPF & STOCK · Eugene, Oregon

SILENCING SATAN
Handbook of Biblical Demonology
13 Studies for Individuals and Groups

Copyright © 2013 Sharon Beekmann. All rights reserved. Except for brief quotations in critical publications or reviews, no part of this book may be reproduced in any manner without prior written permission from the publisher. Write: Permissions, Wipf and Stock Publishers, 199 W. 8th Ave., Suite 3, Eugene, OR 97401.

Wipf & Stock
An Imprint of Wipf and Stock Publishers
199 W. 8th Ave., Suite 3
Eugene, OR 97401
www.wipfandstock.com

ISBN 13: 978-1-62032-731-9
Manufactured in the U.S.A.

Unless otherwise noted, Scripture quotations are taken from the HOLY BIBLE, NEW INTERNATI ONAL VERSION®. Copyright © 1973, 1978, 1984, 2011 by Biblica, Inc. Used by permission of Zondervan. All rights reserved worldwide.

Contents

1 Getting Started: Foreword, Preface, Introduction / 1

2 The Worship of Other Gods: 1–6 / 7

3 Contending with the Demons: 7–13 / 12

4 Bondage of a Magical Worldview: 14–19 / 17

5 God's Faithfulness: 20–22 / 22

6 God Reigns: 23–26 / 27

7 Christ's Kingdom on Earth: 27–31, 53–54 / 31

8 Light Shines in the Darkness: 45–48, 55–56 / 37

9 The Children of God: 32–37 / 42

10 Death Has No Sting: 38–44 / 46

11 The Word Is My Lamp: 49–50 / 51

12 Victory in Jesus: 51–52 / 56

13 Come, Lord Jesus: 57–58 / 61

Appendix A: Leadership Guide for Small Group Leaders / 67

1

Getting Started

Foreword, Preface, Introduction

For he has rescued us from the dominion of darkness and brought us into the kingdom of the Son he loves, in whom we have redemption, the forgiveness of sins. (Col 1:13–14)

EVANGELICAL CHRISTIANS BELIEVE THAT the Bible is *the* authority on spiritual matters in the heavenly and earthly realms. Scripture tells us about God's original intention for creation; what went wrong; and what he has done, is doing, and will do to redeem the damage done. Satan and the demons appear in God's story, but always in the context of God's greater narrative about his glory and sovereignty over his creation. In this regard, Satan and the demons are minor characters, albeit vicious ones, in the biblical narrative. Scripture leaves a lot unsaid about supernatural evil, but God has told us exactly what we need to know. We should not fill gaps in our understanding with information from extra-biblical sources.

Certainly, the most important biblical revelation regarding Satan and the demons is that our Lord Jesus Christ defeated and disarmed them at the cross (Col 1:3; 2:13–15). "The reason the Son of God appeared was to destroy the devil's work" (1 John 3:8). The

Lord Jesus Christ has rescued believers from the kingdom of darkness (Col 1:13). Christians are to single-mindedly focus on Jesus Christ. As they *reach* for the Savior, believers can *resist* demonic influences (Jas 4:7; 1 Pet 5:8–9). Though aware of the demons, believers should keep them in their peripheral vision and focus on Jesus Christ. The Bible sufficiently describes the character, strategies, and tactics of the demons for us to obey this simple directive.

Popular culture would have us believe otherwise. The electronic and print media saturate Western cultures with tantalizing and terrifying depictions of the devil, vampires, ghosts, demons, divination, and magic. Even Christians struggle to distinguish fact from fiction. For example, when believers personally encounter supernatural phenomena such as strong intuitions, voices, visions, or dreams, they tend to rely on conventional wisdom to discern the source. If an experience is uplifting, informative, and applicable to daily life or if a prediction or even a portion of it comes true—the source must be God. Contrarily, if the manifestation is dark and menacing, if the counsel is farfetched and not applicable to daily living, and if nothing foretold comes true—the source must be of either the devil or one's imagination. This conventional wisdom is based on the misconception that evil cannot masquerade as something good and beautiful and that God would not cause someone to feel bad or fearful. The Bible does not support these assumptions and beliefs, and Christians need to know what it does teach.

Years ago I watched George C. Scott play the role of George Patton, the World War II general. Patton stood in a trench in the North African desert gazing at Erwin Rommel's massive army as they marched down a corridor formed by boulders jutting up from the desert floor. Patton had outwitted the Desert Fox. With binoculars pressed against his cheeks, Patton watched balls of fire erupt from exploding tanks and fiery clouds balloon on the desert. Patton smiled and said, "Rommel, I read your book!" Patton knew his enemy's mind, tactics, and character—and so should we.

Does the study of Satan's character and capabilities increase fear or give him too much attention? In fact, when presented from a biblical perspective, such knowledge can increase faith in Jesus Christ and enable Christians to more effectively serve God.

Getting Started

Believers are equipped to resist Satan and to reflexively turn to Jesus Christ who empowers them to stand with him as he redeems the damage done by Satan, who works solely for his vainglory.

ABOUT THE STUDY GUIDE

This study guide is a companion booklet to *Silencing Satan: Handbook of Biblical Demonology*, which I co-authored with Peter G. Bolt. Our goal in writing *Silencing Satan* was to teach the nature, character, capabilities, intent, authority, and strategies of Satan and the demons *within the framework* of the sovereignty and character of God, the Fall, and the gospel of Jesus Christ. In *Silencing Satan* and in this study guide, we approach the Bible through the eyes of faith, believing that God has spoken and is speaking through the people, situations, and events described in it. We believe that the ultimate basis for interpreting Scripture is Scripture itself. This booklet will help you study the Bible references and chapters of *Silencing Satan*.

In both the book and the study guide, we make every effort not to exaggerate Satan's power or incite fears of the dark angels. Jesus Christ defeated them through his life, death, and resurrection, and he clothes his people with himself. You need not fear this evil, "because the one who is in you is greater than the one who is in the world" (1 John 4:4).

The study guide contains thirteen lessons that will help you prayerfully think about, respond to, and apply the material in *Silencing Satan: Handbook of Biblical Demonology*. Approach the lessons with the attitude that God will teach you something about himself, supernatural evil, and Christ's victory over the demons. Each lesson begins with a Bible verse, prayer, and short commentary. The study contains assigned readings and questions to help you think about and apply the material. Write your answers in the spaces provided and close your study with prayer. The lessons can be used in individual or group study.

Silencing Satan

Individual Study

Each lesson has the following format:

1. Pray: Read the opening Scripture and pray. Thank and praise God for what he has done, is doing, and will do on your behalf. Ask him for wisdom and guidance as you study.

2. Begin: Each lesson begins with an introductory commentary. For this introductory lesson, ask yourself, "What questions would I like answered about the demonic realm?

3. Study: Read the assigned chapters and Scripture references. Carefully read the study questions and write your answers in the space provided. Return to the chapter(s) and passages as needed. The assigned reading for this first lesson is the Foreword, Preface, and Introduction of *Silencing Satan*. Record your initial responses to the material.

4. Reflect: Each lesson asks for your personal responses to the study. Reflect on your thoughts and feelings as you completed the lesson.

5. Apply: Relate the lesson to your personal life and ministry situations. Give examples of how you could apply its teachings.

6. Pray: Thank God for his wisdom and guidance. Pray and intercede for others.

Group Study

When using the study guide in a group situation, the leader and members should complete the assigned lesson prior to the meeting. During the meeting, the leader guides the members through the lesson. The leader opens by reading Scripture and praying. The leader or group member paraphrases the commentary and invites responses. Then the group moves through the study and closes in prayer.

Getting Started

The First Meeting

Read the Foreword, Preface, and Introduction of *Silencing Satan* before the first meeting. Open with prayer and discuss the following items. You might paraphrase these guidelines using your own words to convey the intent.

1. Ask group members to introduce themselves and to share their reason(s) for joining the study. Ask whether they have specific questions they would like to have answered.

2. Establish agreement among members about attendance, participation, confidentiality, and preparation. For example, "I agree to make an effort to prepare for and attend meetings. I agree to participate in discussions, to help the group keep on task, and to encourage others to participate. I agree to keep confidential personal information shared in the group."

3. Discuss guidelines for participating in the group.

    a. Productive participation: Productive members come to the group prepared, listen attentively as people talk, try to build on what others say, help the group stay on message, invite silent members to talk, share openly without allowing the discussion to overwhelm the group, and respect the leader. The content of the discussion reflects a healthy balance between comments about Christ's victory over the demonic realm and attributes and activities of Satan and the demons.

    a. Counterproductive participation: Counterproductive members dominate the discussion or refuse to talk, belittle others' comments through sarcasm or innuendo, make dogmatic comments, consistently express skepticism, excessively give advice, and ignore others' contributions. They exaggerate Satan's power and ignore Christ's defeat and dominion over him.

4. Close with prayer and intercede for others.

Silencing Satan

Additional information for leaders is available in Appendix A.
We pray that God will bless you as you progress through these lessons.

Let us hold unswervingly to the hope we profess, for he who promised is faithful. (Heb 10:23)

2

The Worship of Other Gods

1–6

SCRIPTURE

You shall have no other gods before me. You shall not make for yourself an image in the form of anything in heaven above or on the earth beneath or in the waters below. You shall not bow down to them or worship them; for I, the Lord your God, am a jealous God, punishing the children for the sin of the parents to the third and fourth generation of those who hate me, but showing love to a thousand generations of those who love me and keep my commandments. (Deut 5:7–10)

PRAY

BEGIN

PEOPLE OF THE ANCIENT Near East believed that the greater and lesser deities and a host of spirit beings had enormous influence over human existence, for good and for evil. They developed rituals and a class of people known as priests, mediums, witchdoctors, healers, and soothsayers to intermediate on their behalf with the spiritual realm. Religious traditions were embedded in cultures, and the people expended considerable time, talent, and materials contending with the unseen world.

The Mesopotamians, Egyptians, and Canaanites did not know God; biblically, the only other source of spiritual inspiration is Satan. In fact, the gods they worshipped and appeased reflected the character and activity of the demonic realm. The Bible itself identifies the pagan deities as demons. As you begin your study, read Deut 32:17 and Ps 106:37 (a few versions translate the word "demon" as "false god") and 1 Cor 10:20–22, Eph 2:2, Rev 9:20, and John 12:31. Though under demonic influence, God clearly holds the people of these ancient civilizations accountable for the lives they led and the gods they worshipped.

STUDY

Read the Introduction and chapters 1–6 of *Silencing Satan* and the Scripture references.

1. What is animism? (See pages 5 and 13.) Scripture teaches that our Creator God exists separately from his creation. Paraphrase how the biblical worldview differs from an animistic one.

2. People from the Ancient Near East identified a spirit's name by its host, effect or influence, or appearance. For example, there were tree spirits, plague demons, and spirits of the dead. The greater deities embodied and ruled over such things as the seasons, weather, fertility, seas, and death. What did people do with an image of Osiris to increase their crops? Why did they do this?

3. The people appeased the spirits by performing rituals. List ways people dealt with the demons. What motivated the people to perform these rituals? What does it mean that the rituals were *quid pro quo*?

4. The deities and spirits were a mixture of good and evil; they were unpredictable and adhered to no moral code. The people believed that the gods and goddesses engaged in fierce battles that had significant consequences for human existence. Describe the activities of the Egyptian Sekhmet and Canaanite Baal. How might these legends reflect Satan's inspiration?

5. Who was Angra Mainyu of Zoroastrianism and where did he live? How did Zoroastrians avoid going to the underworld as the religion developed?

6. What is astrology? Which passages of Scripture condemn it as divination and star worship?

7. Which two Canaanite gods offered the greatest threat to the Hebrews? El was head god of Canaan, and the Hebrews used "el" in everyday conversation to mean god. Which Hebrew names for God use *El*? What are the dangers of borrowing words from other religions? What are the benefits?

8. Read Exod 20:3 and Deut 5:7–10. In light of the Egyptian and Canaanite beliefs and practices, why was this first commandment so vital to Israelite survival?

REFLECT

9. On a scale from one (don't exist) to ten (do exist) rank your belief in the existence of angelic beings.
   1_____10

10. On a scale from one (don't exist) to ten (do exist) rank your belief in the existence of Satan and the demons.
    1_____10

Record any other thoughts or feelings you had as you completed this study. What most impressed you about the religious beliefs and practices of these cultures?

APPLY

What do the religious beliefs and practices of these ancient Near East people tell us about Satan's character, capabilities, and strategies? How is this study relevant to modern-day Christians? How is it relevant to you?

PRAY

Thank God for his gift of salvation, his wisdom, and guidance. Intercede for others. Contemplate the following verse from Scripture.

Being strengthened with all power according to his glorious might so that you may have great endurance and patience, and giving joyful thanks to the Father, who has qualified you to share in the inheritance of his holy people in the kingdom of light. For he has rescued us from the dominion of darkness and brought us into the kingdom of the Son he loves, in whom we have redemption, the forgiveness of sins. (Col 1:11–14)

3

Contending with the Demons

7–13

SCRIPTURE

So God created mankind in his own image, in the image of God he created them; male and female he created them. God blessed them and said to them, "Be fruitful and increase in number; fill the earth and subdue it." (Gen 1:27–28)

PRAY

BEGIN

DURING THE FOUR HUNDRED years between the Old and New Testaments, people in the ancient Near East developed a complex demonology. Classical and Hellenistic Greek philosophers used the terms *daimon* and "divine" for spiritual beings. Closer to New Testament times, they ranked the *daimon* on a continuum from evil to good. The change was due in part to Plato's philosophical dualism that deemed the physical world evil and the heavenly realities virtuous. After death, spirits of the deceased that were inclined toward the good rose to the heavens. Ones inclined toward evil went downward. The common folk believed that evil demons were spirits of the dead and that they resided in the air close to the earth, in deserted places such as deserts and cemeteries, and in the underworld beneath the ground. Ancient Near East people used rituals to cope with their destructive influences on human beings.

Ancient Near East people feared the demons. They believed that without provocation, demons could possess them, afflict diseases upon them, drive them insane, and torment them day and night. The greater deities were capricious and powerful rulers that controlled all of nature. Many gods and goddesses demonstrated concern by not harming their subjects. The people surely felt inconsequential and vulnerable in light of the gods' great dramas. It's no wonder that they exerted considerable effort to appease the unseen world through rituals and by calling upon professional magicians, witchdoctors, mediums, prophets, and necromancers.

STUDY

Read chapters 7–13 of *Silencing Satan* and the Scripture references.

1. List the Greco-Roman gods and describe their character and activity.

2. How did the people distinguish between genuine and false prophets? Who was Apollonius?

3. What was the Ephesia Grammata? The Delphi Oracle? Who was a "belly talker"? What did "ventriloquist" mean in the ancient Near East?

4. Paraphrase and list the ways pseudepigraphal literature expanded the role of God's holy angels.

5. Describe the exorcism ritual that used Solomon's ring.

6. In this literature, the people named the demon based on its area of influence, such as demon of murder or strife or envy. In the Bible, there is no evidence that demons specialize in particular sins. The ancient Near East people believed that identifying the demon's name gave the exorcist power over him. How does this represent a magical worldview?

7. Apocryphal writings are included in the Roman Catholic Bible. Protestants do not consider them authoritative. Why did the Reformers exclude them from the Protestant Bible?

8. Paraphrase the story of Tobit. The story expands the role of holy and evil angels. How does it diminish God's role in his creation?

9. Describe the origination of demons according to writings in the Dead Sea Scrolls. Give examples of how the writers mixed magic with Old Testament teaching.

REFLECTION

God created humankind in his image. God loves us; he gives dignity to human life. We are important to him, so much so that he sent the Son Jesus Christ to live as a man, to die, and to rise again. Jesus Christ offers salvation to all who believe in him. For a moment, reflect on the radical difference between our Holy God and the gods, goddesses, and demons of ancient Near East cultures. Record some of your thoughts.

APPLY

Ancient Near East people evaluated spiritual experiences based on their appearance, usefulness, and/or accuracy. Give examples of how people use the same criteria today.

PRAY

Thank God for his gift of salvation, and for his wisdom and guidance. Intercede for others.

4

Bondage of a Magical Worldview

14–19

SCRIPTURE

After this, the word of the LORD came to Abram in a vision. "Do not be afraid, Abram. I am your shield, your very great reward."
(Gen 15:1)

PRAY

BEGIN

THE RELIGIONS OF THE ancient Near East offered little solace to the people. Without provocation, unseen forces threatened their lives through possession, curses, and harassing ghosts. The people had no authoritative scriptures and so relied on traditions and personal experiences to understand these supernatural beings. The high drama of demons transfixed the people. Sadly, deceiving spirits spewed lies and half-truths about the spiritual realm and the human condition. People performed mindless rituals and solicited professionals to persuade the spirits not to hurt them.

People believed that the strong dominated the weak in the heavens and on earth. In the heavens, the great gods warred and the winners restored harmony or produced more chaos. Great gods could stop the demons from annihilating humanity. On earth, people clustered in tribes with patriarchal authority structures and strictly prescribed roles. The primary concern was strengthening and preserving the tribe, and in this regard, individual needs and desires were inconsequential.

God formed a nation, the Israelites, amid these cultures and introduced a religion that effectively upended the animistic, magical worldview of the ancient Near East. God revealed his righteousness and commanded his people to obey his moral laws. Yahweh was their authority and power. They were to obey him and rely on him—not on magical words, rituals, and professional demon-destroyers.

STUDY

Read chapters 14–19 of *Silencing Satan* and the Scripture references.

1. The rituals and paraphernalia of the ancient exorcists reflected their magical worldview. Words had power, certain objects contained power, and naming a spirit gave the exorcist power over the demon. List the steps of an ancient Near East exorcism.

Bondage of a Magical Worldview

2. The Old Testament does not describe or prescribe rituals for exorcisms. Hebrew rituals came from extra-biblical writings, e.g., pseudepigraphal writings and the Dead Sea Scrolls. How did Hebrew exorcisms differ from pagan ones?

3. Are demonized people portrayed as active or passive participants in pagan exorcisms?

4. Who and what is Hades? What is Sheol? What is the underworld?

5. What is the cult of ancestors (also see page 6)? Did Israel participate in the cult of ancestors or consult the dead? Read Isa 8:19–20. What is the prophet saying?

6. Paraphrase the story of the man with an omen. How does belief in omens enslave and keep people in bondage?

7. What was a curse in ancient Near East cultures? What is a curse in the Bible? Who alone is able to curse and bless? Why should Christians not fear curses from occultists?

8. An animistic worldview undermines people's ability to problem-solve and act decisively. Paraphrase and respond to Paul Hiebert's quote on page 57.

REFLECT

Scripture tells us that God is our shield and very great reward. He saves us from sin and from obsessively performing rituals that lead to deeper bondage. He gives us himself. We praise our Lord Jesus Christ for his gift of salvation. Record your thoughts and feelings about his gift of salvation. What most impressed you in this study?

APPLY

Identify some superstitions and omens that are supported in modern day culture. Is the modern church susceptible to animistic practices? Identify some films in popular culture that are based on animism and a magical worldview.

PRAY

Praise God for his gift of the Son Jesus Christ who offers salvation to the world. Intercede for others.

5

God's Faithfulness

20–22

SCRIPTURE

If you say, "The LORD is my refuge," and you make the Most High your dwelling, no harm will overtake you, no disaster will come near your tent. For he will command his angels concerning you to guard you in all your ways; they will lift you up in their hands, so that you will not strike your foot against a stone. You will tread on the lion and the cobra; you will trample the great lion and the serpent. (Psalm 91:9–13)

PRAY

BEGIN

MOST OLD TESTAMENT REFERENCES to Satan and the demons occur in the context of human rebellion against God. In the opening chapters of Genesis, Satan uses the serpent to tempt Adam and Eve

God's Faithfulness

to be unfaithful to God. As God curses him to a humiliating existence, Satan does not utter a word. In the Old Testament canon, the *satan* is referenced three times, and God's prophets mention the demons when they confront Israelite participation in idolatry, divination, and other forbidden practices. The demons are complicit in Israelites' rebellion against God.

God's prohibitions protected his people from the demons; their rebellion put them in harm's way. God had formed the nation of Israel for his glory and to accomplish his purposes. God blessed them when they loved and obeyed him and judged them when they rebelled against him. God was their hope, for he reigned over his creation—including the demons. The apocryphal writings tend to portray God as a distant figure who sends holy angels to engage in bitter battles with evil angels after they ravaged humanity. Old Testament Yahweh personally provides for, protects, and watches over his people.

STUDY

Read chapters 20–22, and the Scripture references.

1. The Old Testament rarely mentions Satan and the demons, though it affirms their existence. On what and on whom were God's people to focus?

2. The Old Testament associates demons with idolatry and wastelands. Paraphrase Zechariah's judgment and foretelling that one day God would set this right. Who fulfilled this prophecy?

3. God silenced the Egyptian magicians when he delivered his people from bondage. How does this event depict God's sovereign reign over Satan and the demons?

4. God's strongest judgment of Israel and Judah was due to their participation in necromancy (talking to the dead) and other forbidden practices. Why is listening to and relying on Satan and the demons such an affront to God?

5. List the ways that ancient Near East cultures used snakes and serpents to symbolize instruments of evil, the magical arts, and chaos.

6. List the biblical support for Satan being the moral agent that inspired the serpent.

God's Faithfulness

7. List the seven characteristics of Satan and his abilities that are implied in Genesis 3:1.

8. Satan calls God a liar and accuses God of being envious of his knowledge and power. Who actually is envious? Human beings are *not* designed to be morally autonomous or to be like God. Paraphrase Satan's deception.

9. God judges Satan and his fate is sealed. What God decrees, he will bring about! Do you believe this?

REFLECT

Read and contemplate Psalm 91. Reflect on the faithfulness of God. Did you personally learn anything new about Satan and his practices from this study?

APPLY

Read the Christian application story on pages 73–74. What would you say to the young man? Satan and the demons use people and our culture to instigate rebellion against God. Identify other examples.

PRAY

Praise God for his protection and provision in our daily lives. Intercede for others.

6

God Reigns

23–26

SCRIPTURE

Hear, O Israel: The LORD our God, the LORD is one. Love the LORD your God with all your heart and with all your soul and with all your strength. (Deut 6:4–5)

PRAY

BEGIN

THE OLD TESTAMENT IS a story about God and the nation of Israel that God formed for the fulfillment of his purposes and for his glory. The early Hebrews attributed all events in heaven and on earth to him. God sent such things as evil spirits, droughts, famines, holy angels, and prosperity. The Old Testament leaves much unexplained about what transpires in the spiritual realm, and it does not reveal the reasons for and the extent of demonic influences in human affairs. Occasionally, God pulls back the curtain for us to glimpse heavenly realities. In Job, we learn about Satan's participation in the heavenly council when he bargains with God to attack Job. In 1 Samuel, we read that an evil spirit from the Lord incapacitates Saul and that Saul communicates with the spirit called Samuel when he visits the witch at Endor. We learn that Sheol is the Hebrew underworld, an ill-defined place for the dead that exists beneath the earth. Christians understand that God's sovereignty extends to the living and the dead, and that Satan and his demons never have final say on heavenly or earthly matters.

STUDY

Read chapters 23–26 and the Scripture references.

1. King Saul disobeyed God, and God rejected him as king. God withdrew the Holy Spirit, and an evil spirit afflicted Saul. How did Saul's behavior change? What does this tell us about what demons can and cannot do?

2. Saul and his servants believed a demon afflicted Saul. Can a demon cause symptoms of mental illness? Can a person have a demon and be mentally ill?

3. Ancient Near East people believed that spirits of the dead communicated through mediums—a practice called necromancy.

The medium was "on familiar terms" with the spirit that appeared as the dead, and they called it a "familiar spirit." Demons can masquerade as the dead. List passages in Scripture that forbid the practice of necromancy.

4. The Old and New Testaments affirm that people afflicted with demons fight by maintaining a right relationship with God. After the opening chapters of Job, Satan is not heard of again. The story is about Job's relationship with God. What does this book teach us about resisting Satan even when we are severely assaulted?

5. What does the story of Job teach us about what Satan can and cannot do?

6. The final chapters of Job (38–42) reveal the majesty and power of our Creator God. What do we learn about God?

7. In what ways does Sheol in the Old Testament differ from modern-day conceptions of hell?

REFLECT

Christians cannot fully understand spiritual realities, and we trust God to defend, strengthen, and protect us. Meditate on Deut 6:4–5. Contemplate these verses and write your response.

What other thoughts and feelings did you have as you completed this study?

APPLY

What would you say to someone who suspects that a demon torments him or her? The symptoms of demonic affliction and psychiatric illness are similar, and some people may be afflicted by both. How should we pray for such people? What would you say to someone who consults mediums or relies on astrology?

PRAY

Praise God as Lord of heaven and earth and of the living and the dead. Intercede for others.

7

Christ's Kingdom on Earth

27–31, 53–54

SCRIPTURE

And having disarmed the powers and authorities, he made a public spectacle of them, triumphing over them by the cross. (Col 2:15)

PRAY

BEGIN

SATAN AND THE DEMONS emerge from the shadows as Jesus begins his earthly ministry. Satan appears in the wilderness, demon-tormented people come to Jesus, and Satan inspires Jesus's enemies and infiltrates his inner circle. Even so, Satan and the demons are minor characters in the Gospel narratives. God's purpose in mentioning them is to demonstrate the power of God as revealed through the Son Jesus Christ. Satan and the demons are foils in

God's greater story of bringing the way of salvation to humankind. The Messianic era has dawned!

Shortly before his crucifixion, Jesus saw Satan fall like lightning from heaven (Luke 10:18), and he announced that Satan would be driven from this world (John 12:31). Jesus understood that when he died in substitutionary atonement for human sin and rose from the dead, he effectively disarmed Satan and the demons. In his parables, Jesus warned the people that their spiritual enemy was malicious and conniving, but one day Satan and the demons would receive punishment both terrifying and just.

Until the great Day of the Lord, Satan and the demons work hard to disrupt God's relationships with his people. Their assaults come regularly and sometimes with great force. Jesus the Good Shepherd offers care for his sheep and protection from supernatural predators. Jesus gives his people divine armor that protects them from Satan's attacks. Jesus enables them to stand their ground and resist the devil. This is true when the enemy tempts them to sin and when he inspires supernatural phenomena such as visions and dreams.

STUDY

Read chapters 27–31, 53–54 and the Scripture references.

1. Where do Satan and demons reside according to the people in Jesus's day?

2. Does God use his holy angels to battle Satan and the demons? See page 94. Who defeated the demons? When did he defeat them?

3. List the ways Satan and the demons came against Jesus during his earthly ministry.

4. What do we learn about Satan in the Parable of the Sower? When is he most active?

5. What do we learn about Satan in the Parable of the Weeds? When will God ultimately judge Satan and his followers?

6. What do we learn about Satan and the demons in the Parable of the Sheep and Goats? This New Testament passage specifically states that Satan in some manner oversees fallen angels or demons. What is their fate?

7. What do we learn about demons in the Parable of the Restless Demon? What must the man do to prevent demons from tormenting him?

8. God gives his people divine armor to withstand demonic attacks. Believers are to clothe themselves with Jesus. List the pieces of the armor and what they represent.

9. Most of the armor is for defensive purposes. The only weapon that is both defensive *and* offensive is the sword of the Spirit, which is the "words" of God. Why is the sword of the Spirit the most powerful weaponry of God?

10. Believers should test the source of supernatural phenomena. What does the acronym TESTS stand for?

11. God redeemed the evil that Satan inflicted on two girls when they clung to Jesus and his Word. List the elements in their story that speak to Jesus's victory over evil.

12. Jesus is Lord in heaven and on earth. Believers resist Satan by turning to and giving authority to Jesus and his Word rather than to their experiences. Why is this so difficult to do?

REFLECT

The cross is the quintessential symbol of Christian faith. Believers in Christ are God's children, and he protects his own! He may not immediately remove us from or resolve difficult situations, but he does enable us to stand with him midst them—as he deals with the enemy of our soul. Paraphrase what this means to you.

APPLY

Perhaps you have experienced a supernatural event, but even if you have not, list the ways you could apply the teaching in this lesson. How do you clothe yourself with Jesus? How do you stand with Jesus in the face of adversity?

PRAY

Contemplate the following verse from Scripture.

Finally, be strong in the Lord and in his mighty power. Put on the full armor of God, so that you can take your stand against the devil's schemes. For our struggle is not against flesh and blood, but against the rulers, against the authorities, against the powers of this dark world and against the spiritual forces of evil in the heavenly realms. Therefore put on the full armor of God, so that when the day of evil comes, you may be able to stand your ground, and after you have done everything, to stand. Stand firm then, with the belt of truth buckled around your waist, with the breastplate of righteousness in place, and with your feet fitted with the readiness that comes from the gospel of peace. In addition to all this, take up the shield of faith, with which you can extinguish all the flaming arrows of the evil one. Take the helmet of salvation and the sword of the Spirit, which is the word of God.

And pray in the Spirit on all occasions with all kinds of prayers and requests. With this in mind, be alert and always keep on praying for all the Lord's people. (Eph 6:10–18)

Thank God for his protection, wisdom, and guidance.
Intercede for others.

8

Light Shines in the Darkness

45–48, 55–56

SCRIPTURE

No, in all these things we are more than conquerors through him who loved us. For I am convinced that neither death nor life, neither angels nor demons, neither the present nor the future, nor any powers, neither height nor depth, nor anything else in all creation, will be able to separate us from the love of God that is in Christ Jesus our Lord. (Rom 8:37–39)

PRAY

BEGIN

WHEN JESUS BEGAN HIS earthly ministry, the kingdom of God came in power and Satan's power was severely curtailed. The light of Jesus shone into darkness, and darkness could not overcome it (John 1:5). Jesus proclaimed the truth and it upended Satan's lies and pretentions. The purposes of God always prevailed! Even so, Satan and the demons looked for opportunities to turn people from God by tempting them not to love God and not to believe that his way was the best and only way for salvation.

This lesson focuses on three tactics of Satan and the demons. One, they inspire the worship of creatures and created things rather than of the Creator (Rom 1:25). The consistent message of Scripture is that God hates idolatry and that he alone is to be worshipped. Two, they afflict and inhabit human beings and cause unbearable suffering in order to create doubt about God's goodness and sovereignty. Jesus utters a command, the kingdom of God comes in power, and the demons flee. Jesus came to set captives free!

Three, demons inspire teachings that encourage immorality and deny that Jesus came from God and that he is the Christ (1 Tim 4:1). God's people respond by speaking the Word boldly. Jesus rules everything, including the forces of evil, principalities, and powers. God's people have nothing to fear, for they are anchored in the assurance that nothing separates us from the love of God (Rom 8:37–39).

When demons afflict or manifest, believers should immediately call out, "Jesus! Come, Lord Jesus." Our deliverance does not depend on tremendous faith but on whether we willfully and unwaveringly depend on Jesus Christ who is the object of our faith and our source of strength. He removes the demons and changes us from the inside out to reflect himself.

STUDY

Read chapters 45–48, 55–56 and the Scripture references.

1. Biblically, what is idolatry? God soundly punished the Israelites for their idolatrous practices. Idolatry can take many forms such as greed for material goods, prestige, and power. John closes his letter, "Dear children, keep yourselves from idols" (1 John 5:21). What does this mean to you?

2. The Bible portrays the demoniacs as victims of demonic torment and control. The people are "in" or "have" an impure spirit (demon) that coerces them into submission. Did Jesus require a confession of sin or ask them to profess faith in him before removing the demons?

3. Theologically, who has legitimate authority and power over heaven and earth? How do the stories of the demoniacs foreshadow or point to Jesus's gift of salvation and Satan's ultimate defeat?

4. Who is the antichrist? Who are the antichrists? Their primary strategy is to falsify the Word of God. Give examples. When are the "last days"?

5. Principalities and powers are general terms for forces of evil in the heavenly realm. Christians do not have to identify demons' names and hierarchy in order to deal with them. Why is this so? Who had dealt with them? How did he do it?

Silencing Satan

6. List the four criteria of conventional wisdom for evaluating a psychic's authenticity. Scripture forbids all forms of divination. Why?

7. What does Scripture say about talking to the dead? Though first century people believed that spirits of the dead tormented the living, Jesus treats them as demons in league with the devil. If the dead appear, what should Christians do?

8. In chapter 56, Jesus Christ removed the demons when people maintained a clear-eyed focus on Jesus and Scripture. Record your responses to their stories.

REFLECT

Supernatural phenomena such as communications with the dead, voices, and visions startle and transfix us. Have you had a supernatural encounter? People are often reluctant to talk about them, though they are rarely forgotten. Reflect on the stories and teachings of this lesson, and record your thoughts and feelings.

APPLY

How would you minister to someone who has encountered supernatural evil? Ask our Lord Jesus Christ to shine his light in your heart and identify any idols in your life. Prayerfully, confess your sin and praise God.

PRAY

Thank God for his wisdom and guidance and intercede for others. Meditate on the following:

No, in all these things we are more than conquerors through him who loved us. For I am convinced that neither death nor life, neither angels nor demons, neither the present nor the future, nor any powers, neither height nor depth, nor anything else in all creation, will be able to separate us from the love of God that is in Christ Jesus our Lord. (Rom 8:37–39)

9

The Children of God

32–37

SCRIPTURE

Who will bring any charge against those whom God has chosen? It is God who justifies. (Rom 8:33)

PRAY

BEGIN

THE HEAD DEMON IS known by many names and each one describes his influence on human beings. Collectively, these names depict a supernatural being that is abject evil. He has no truth or goodness in him. Believers have the assurance that Jesus Christ disarmed him at the cross and sanctifies believers in righteous living. Believers are sinners saved by grace who base their righteousness on the righteousness of Jesus Christ.

The names of the head demon reflect his character and activities in human and heavenly affairs. Satan is the transliteration of the Hebrew noun *satan* that means adversary and accuser. Satan relentlessly accuses God's people of wrongdoing. The Greek noun *diabolos* from which "devil" is derived means slanderer and accuser. Slander is often malicious, illegitimate, and baseless. The devil slandered Job and even impugned God's character in order to justify ruining Job's life. Jesus referred to Satan as the Evil One in his prayers, and the title effectively contrasts the holiness of God with the evilness of Satan. The Evil One opposes holy God in thought, word, and deed and seeks ways to harm followers of Christ.

Jesus and the people of his day understood that Beelzeboul/bub was a synonym for Satan. The Pharisees accused Jesus of serving Beelzeboul/bub, which was a charge of sorcery. The title Dragon, Serpent of Old in Revelation (12:9; 20:2) has theological significance. Satan inspired the serpent in Genesis 3 that led the first couple astray. The dragon in Revelation 20:2 is bound by an angel of the Lord for a thousand years at the end of which he is thrown into the lake of burning sulfur for eternal torment (v. 10).

Believers put on the full armor of God so they can resist Satan—the devil, the Evil One, the serpent. Though he waits for the opportune time to physically harm, accuse, or slander them, they stand with the Savior of the world in anticipation of the great day when God will silence Satan forever and believers of all time will reign with Jesus Christ in the new heaven and new earth.

STUDY

Read chapters 32–37 and the Scripture references.

1. Give biblical examples of Satan acting as prosecutor, adversary, and accuser. Why did the accuser have no hold on Jesus? (John 14:30)

2. Give biblical examples of the devil acting as the slanderer. What does the title tell us about the devil's character? Contrast the devil's character with that of Jesus who "committed no sin and no deceit was found in his mouth" (1 Pet 2:22).

3. Review the biblical references in which Jesus, John, and Paul use the title Evil One. What makes this title so apt?

4. Sorcery and witchcraft were commonplace in the first-century ancient Near East. What is the significance of the Pharisees accusing Jesus of using Beelzeboul/bub for his source of power?

5. In Revelation 12, the Dragon is enraged by Jesus's victory, and he knows his time is short. What should be our response? See James 4:7.

REFLECT

Have you ever experienced a slanderous or adversarial attack? If so, how did you respond? How would you respond now? Satan accuses and slanders us because we belong to God. He hates the righteousness of Christ, and he hates us. Yet, we need not be afraid, for we belong to the One who rules heaven and earth. Reflect on the teachings of this lesson. Which teachings have been most significant to you?

APPLY

The titles of Satan tell us about him and the ways he might try to influence us not to trust and love God as we should. When we feel unjustly accused or slandered, we should remember who we are in Christ. We are children of God! Identify ways you can apply what you have learned in this lesson in your daily life.

PRAY

Thank God for his protection and provision in your life and intercede for others. Prayerfully contemplate the following:

Who will bring any charge against those whom God has chosen? It is God who justifies. Who then is the one who condemns? No one. Christ Jesus who died—more than that, who was raised to life—is at the right hand of God and is also interceding for us. (Rom 8:33–34)

10

Death Has No Sting

38–44

SCRIPTURE

I pray that the eyes of your heart may be enlightened in order that you may know the hope to which he has called you, the riches of his glorious inheritance in his holy people, and his incomparably great power for us who believe. That power is the same as the mighty strength he exerted when he raised Christ from the dead and seated him at his right hand in the heavenly realms, far above all rule and authority, power and dominion, and every name that is invoked, not only in the present age but also in the one to come. (Eph 1:18–21)

PRAY

BEGIN

JESUS CHRIST RULES OVER Satan and the demons—he always has and always will. Satan has presumed authority that he acquires by lacing God's truth with lies. He deceives people who are ignorant of God and Scripture and then inspires them to reflect his twisted image. He also tempts people who know God and Scripture. In the wilderness, he tempted Jesus to turn stones into bread to satisfy his hunger. Jesus understood that eating when hungry was not inherently sinful nor was performing a miracle. Jesus would later miraculously feed thousands with a few loaves of bread and some fish. Disobeying God was a sin. God the Father would determine when Jesus ended his fast and when he would perform miracles. A miracle in the service of Satan was sin.

The names of Satan speak to his nature and activities. He is the Tempter, Father of Lies, the Deceiver, Prince of Demons, one with the Power of Death, Murderer, and Destroyer. His titles alert us to his hatred of God and human beings. He wants us to further *his* purposes on earth. He wants human beings to fear death and to suffer his fate of eternal torment. Christians know that Jesus gives them eternal life; death has lost its sting. Satan is not God. Satan does not rule the heavens and earth—God does. Believers fight the devil by maintaining relational harmony with God. They resist Satan just as Jesus did in the wilderness. When the light of Jesus Christ shines on the fruit of his work, Satan's pretensions collapse like a house of cards.

STUDY

Read chapters 38–44 and the Scripture references.

1. Satan's temptations are not always to do something inherently sinful, but to do something outside the will of God. Apply this principle to Satan's three temptations of Jesus in the wilderness.

2. The subtleties of Satan's temptations mask his lethal intentions. The Father of Lies deceives in order to enslave and kill. Give examples from Scripture.

3. False teachers appear wise because they appeal to human processes and desires. Give an example(s) from Scripture.

4. The title Prince of Demons implies that a head demon leads a group of demons. People in Jesus's day called Satan the Prince of Demons. Satan and the demons are united in their opposition to God, but they may not be well organized. What is the support for this position?

5. Explain the ways that Satan has the power of death.

6. Christians believe that God alone has the power over life and death, but Satan is called the Murderer. Who does he use to do his evil deeds? Give biblical examples.

7. Who is the Destroyer? Are the destroying angels in the Bible God's holy angels or Satan and the demons?

REFLECT

Are you aware of a time when God tested your faithfulness to him? The devil's temptations are not always to do something inherently sinful but to do something outside of the will of God. Have you experienced such a temptation? Satan desires our death, but Jesus Christ gives us new life now and for eternity. Death has lost its sting! Reflect on your thoughts and feelings as you completed this lesson.

APPLY

Satan is a formidable enemy because he supports our natural inclination to sin. He tempts people to be immoral. Though Satan inspires sin, God holds human beings accountable for who they are and how they behave. Identify practical applications of this lesson to your life and ministry?

PRAY

Thank God for his protection and provision in your life. Intercede for others. Prayerfully, contemplate the following Scripture.

I pray that the eyes of your heart may be enlightened in order that you may know the hope to which he has called you, the riches of his glorious inheritance in his holy people, and his incomparably great power for us who believe. That power is the same as the mighty strength he exerted when he raised Christ from the dead and seated him at his right hand in the heavenly realms, far above all rule and authority, power and dominion, and every name that is invoked, not only in the present age but also in the one to come. (Eph 1:18–21)

11

The Word Is My Lamp

49–50

SCRIPTURE

The reason the Son of God appeared was to destroy the devil's work. (1 John 3:8)

PRAY

BEGIN

THROUGHOUT CHURCH HISTORY, THEOLOGIANS, monks, pastors, and laity have struggled to understand what Satan and the demons can and cannot do and how Christians should deal with them. As they developed their traditions, many Christian theologians and church leaders drew from extra-biblical writing to fill in gaps in biblical revelation about the demons. They also borrowed from the conventional wisdom of popular cultures. The pendulum swung from exaggerating demonic powers and capabilities to reducing them to mere symbols of human and institutional evil.

Most theologians and evangelists of the first-century church taught that Jesus Christ defeated Satan and the demons at the cross. Christians fought the good fight by bringing people to Jesus Christ, loving and obeying God, and resisting demonic influences. The pendulum soon swung toward giving the demons more power and influence. Faith in Jesus Christ, loving and obeying him seemed insufficient for dealing with demons; more was needed. The expanded demonology effectively diminished God's sovereignty and Christ's work for us at the cross. By the end of the second century, segments of Christendom performed exorcisms prior to baptisms. After Rome fell, monks fled to the desert to live in solitude. They pursued God, resisted sin, and battled demons to become Christ-like.

Fascination with demonic power and influence reached its apex in the Middle Ages when the Inquisition mercilessly tortured heretics whom they defined as servants of Satan. Authorities insisted that attaining confessions through torture served the greater good of purifying the church. Heretics were initially defined as believers who challenged church authority and traditions, but the net gradually expanded to encompass Jews, Muslims, Gypsies, the insane, sleepwalkers, and even popes, monks, and nuns.

Amid this maelstrom, Reformers Martin Luther and John Calvin returned to the theology of the early church fathers and preached that believers were justified through faith in Jesus Christ. Jesus disarmed the demons at the cross and enabled believers to withstand demonic temptations and assaults. No more was needed. Jesus Christ ruled Satan and the demons and he protected and enabled believers to stand with him and against the devil's schemes.

STUDY

1. Who are the two sources of spiritual inspiration in heaven and on earth?

2. Summarize Augustine's description of Satan and the demons. According to early church leaders, how did demons influence daily life? How were they defeated?

3. What did Antony believe about the demons and Christian growth? How did Antony fight the demons?

4. The monks sought solitude in the desert to pursue Christ-likeness. They believed that fighting demons helped them achieve Christian piety. What are the strengths and weaknesses of their position?

5. In the twelfth and thirteenth centuries, scholarly men argued that anyone who opposed church doctrine and traditions was an instrument of the devil. The Inquisition justified torture because it served a greater good, which was to purify the church from heretics. Identify the factors that permitted and even enabled the church to perpetuate this evil.

6. In late medieval times, theologians argued for Satan's irrelevance. What happened in the popular culture?

7. What roles did John Wycliffe and Jan Hus play in the Reformation? What happened to them?

8. What did Luther and Calvin believe about the demons relevant to the gospel of Jesus Christ?

9. Luther said that when he heard noises in the night and realized it was Satan, he turned over and went to sleep. What does this story tell us about Luther's belief about demons and faith in Christ?

10. The Reformers re-established belief in the authority of Scripture as the revealed Word of God. How did this influence their demonology?

REFLECT

Ignoring or aggrandizing Satan's existence and power undermine the authority of Scripture and the atoning sacrifice and resurrection of Jesus Christ. What most impressed you about the teachings and practices of the church during the early church, medieval period, and the Reformation?

APPLY

Popular cultures in Western countries are increasingly fascinated with Satan, demons, occult phenomena, and all things supernatural. What are some examples? How should Christians respond?

PRAY

Thank God for his protection and provision in your life and intercede for others.

12

Victory in Jesus

51–52

SCRIPTURE

Be alert and of sober mind. Your enemy the devil prowls around like a roaring lion looking for someone to devour. Resist him, standing firm in the faith, because you know that the family of believers throughout the world is undergoing the same kind of sufferings. (1 Pet 5:8–9)

PRAY

BEGIN

THE AGE OF REASON dawned and enlightened thinkers began to challenge all things supernatural, including stories in the Bible. They asserted that Satan and demons were myths and symbols of evil. They redefined miracles and other supernatural phenomena as events that science could not yet explain or were simply unknowable. A twentieth-century missiologist lamented that it was as if God did not act in history.

Leaders of the holiness movement and Methodist preachers of the mid-1800s countered that the Spirit of God worked in believers' lives. Faithful Christians could have complete victory over sin, but Satan and the demons worked against them. Pentecostalism was born in the early 1900s and faith healers and pastors performed healing revivals in which they cast out demons and loosened the demons' hold on Christians. Pentecostal and charismatic preachers put spiritual warfare at the center of their theology, and spiritual warfare became synonymous with biblical demonology.

They taught Christian warriors to clothe themselves in the armor of God and rout the enemy through prayer and encounters with supernatural evil. They battled an army of demons with specialized functions that gained access, established strongholds, and thwarted growth in Christ. They believed that demons established strongholds through personal and ancestral sins, occult involvements, sexual and physical abuse, and curses. They robbed believers of joy!

In the twentieth and early twenty-first centuries, most theologians, pastors, and Bible teachers of mainline denominations remained silent on the influences of the demonic realm. Popular culture filled the void with fascinating stories about the devil and the supernatural realm. Film, print, television, and electronic industries unleashed a plethora of books, films, video games, television shows, and talk-show discussions on demon possession, magic, divination, angels, talking with the dead, and heavenly wars between good and evil spiritual powers. New Age and Eastern religious thought and occult practices entered mainstream cultures.

Many evangelical pastors rejected charismatic theology and warned that the warfare metaphor put too much attention on Satan. It misrepresented God's sovereignty over heaven and earth, human culpability for sin, and Jesus Christ's atonement for sin through his sacrificial death on the cross. They argued the traditional evangelical position, which states that Satan was disarmed as a consequence of Jesus's sinless life, death, and resurrection. Jesus Christ sat at the right hand of the Father where he was superior to the angels and had authority over them (Heb 1:3–4). Jesus Christ gave believers a right relationship with God through faith in him. Believers fought Satan and the demons through proclamation, witness, resistance, and humbly loving God and others.

STUDY

Read chapters 51–52 and the Scripture references.

1. The goal of the enlightened philosophers was to free people from superstition and religious dogma through reason and science. Do you believe that reason and Christian faith are incompatible?

2. What did the enlightened philosophers and nineteenth- and twentieth-century theologians believe about Satan and the demons?

3. How did the Pentecostal church and the charismatic movement begin?

4. Describe the influence of modern missionaries on the charismatic movement.

5. Summarize Paul Hiebert's message to mainline churches.

6. Charismatic Christians believe that demons establish strongholds and have the right to assault and harass believers. According to them, how are believers freed? See pages 186–189.

7. Identify the animistic influences in Pentecostal and Charismatic beliefs and practices in regard to the demons.

8. God protects, sustains, nurtures, and guides his people while he furthers his purposes on earth for his glory. God protects us from the demons. Yet, we must do our part. According to the traditional evangelical position, how should believers fight the demons?

REFLECT

Twenty-first-century Christians have been significantly influenced by scientific advancements and enlightened thought. Many people deny Satan's existence and accept the possibility of demonic involvement only when rational explanations cannot account for them, such as genocides and the Holocaust. This lesson emphasizes that both denying his existence and aggrandizing his power diminish what Christ did for us through his life, death, and resurrection. Reflect on this and record your thoughts and feelings.

APPLY

Satan tempts us to mistrust God, and he uses false teachers, supernatural phenomena, temptations to sin, and enticements from the world. Give examples, and record how you can apply the teachings in this lesson to your life.

Pray
Thank God for his protection and provision in your life and intercede for others. Prayerfully, contemplate the following Scripture.

"God opposes the proud but shows favor to the humble." Humble yourselves, therefore, under God's mighty hand, that he may lift you up in due time. Cast all your anxiety on him because he cares for you.

Be alert and of sober mind. Your enemy the devil prowls around like a roaring lion looking for someone to devour. Resist him, standing firm in the faith, because you know that the family of believers throughout the world is undergoing the same kind of sufferings. (1 Pet 5b–9)

13

Come, Lord Jesus

57–58

SCRIPTURE

Dear friends, do not believe every spirit, but test the spirits to see whether they are from God, because many false prophets have gone out into the world. (1 John 4:1)

PRAY

BEGIN

PEOPLE REMEMBER SUPERNATURAL ENCOUNTERS such as hearing a voice, sensing a presence, seeing a vision or spirit, or having strong intuitions that seem right and true. Whether pleasing or terrifying, the experience tends to disorient with its abrupt beginning and ending and otherworldly feel. People put such an event in the back of their minds until someone asks, "Have you ever experienced something supernatural?" Then it is instantly retrieved as if it happened yesterday.

Many Christians tend to assume that information and insights obtained from spiritual sources are superior to those attained by regular problem-solving processes. In this last lesson, we emphasize the importance of testing the source of spiritual phenomena, even when the experience is positive and uplifting and seems wise and true. Test the spirit when the information is personally received or conveyed by well-intentioned, loving people.

Many Western alternative health practices are based on a Hindu worldview that is incompatible with a biblical worldview. People are encouraged to enter altered states of consciousness with the goal of transcending themselves and merging with the life force. The life force allegedly concentrates in chakras along the spine and flows through energy channels that traverse the body to animate and sustain life. They believe that when the flow is unobstructed, people experience harmony with the universal life force. When the flow is blocked, disease and a range of emotional and spiritual problems occur. People can supposedly restore harmony and health through spiritual practices.

Most people who participate in Eastern meditation, yoga, and alternative healing practices ignore or are ignorant of the Hindu influences. In this lesson, we warn casual and serious practitioners that the spiritual realm they enter is not neutral and that the insights, revelation, and visions they experience may well come from demons and not from God the Holy Spirit. We teach that one should not evaluate a practice based on its effectiveness but on the source of inspiration.

The Bible leaves much unsaid about the spiritual realm, but God has told us all we need to know. He saved, is saving, and will save us when we believe in Jesus Christ, the Lord and Savior and Ruler of heavens and earth. He gives us peace when we repent of sins. He redeems and sanctifies us when we worship and praise him in a community of faith. God works on, in, and through his creation; amazingly, he uses us to accomplish his great purposes. One day he will wipe away all our tears (Rev 21:4). Come, Lord Jesus.

Come, Lord Jesus

STUDY

Read chapters 57–58 and the Scripture references.

1. Identify two biblical principles in the story of Saul and Ananias in Acts 9:10–18 that help us evaluate the source of visions.

2. We use the acronym TESTS to describe the process of testing the spirit. Give a real or hypothetical example of how one tests the spirit.

3. Do you believe that Christians should visualize Jesus and talk to him? Why or why not?

4. How should you respond to a Christian who conveys counsel he or she received from God that pertains to your situation?

5. A spiritual practice may alleviate troublesome symptoms, but that does not mean the spiritual source is God. Explain how Claudia's techniques resembled animism and mediumship more than Christ-centered, biblical principles.

6. What two Hindu beliefs entered mainstream Western cultures in the second half of the twentieth century? Identify examples that are widely accepted in our culture.

7. Summarize the differences between Christianity and Hinduism.

8. What are the differences between Christian meditation and Eastern meditation?

9. Explain the positions that the authors take on acupressure (energy manipulation) and yoga.

10. Read and contemplate Rev 21:3–4. God is with us now and is redeeming our lives. On the Day of the Lord, God will completely restore his creation to reflect his glory. Come, Lord Jesus.

Come, Lord Jesus

REFLECT

The effectiveness of occult or Hindu practices is often the most difficult obstacle to accepting the biblical worldview. The practices can relieve pain, vitalize the body, convey insights, or result in a semblance of peace. Reflect on what you thought and felt as you completed this study.

APPLY

Consider how you might use TESTS as you dialogue with Christians who are involved in practices that might be demonically inspired?

PRAY

Thank God for his protection and provision in your life and intercede for others. Praise God and express gratitude for his gift of salvation and deliverance from the Evil One. Prayerfully, contemplate the following Scripture.

He who testifies to these things says, "Yes, I am coming soon." Amen. Come, Lord Jesus. The grace of the Lord Jesus be with God's people. Amen. (Rev 22:20–21)

Appendix A

Leadership Guide for Small Group Leaders

THEOLOGY OF LEADERSHIP

THE PASTORAL METAPHOR OF a shepherd with his sheep had rich theological and cultural significance in ancient Israel. The people routinely saw shepherds tending sheep, and biblical writers used the shepherd metaphor to describe God's faithful care and protection of his people (Ps 23). Jesus applied the image to himself in two of his "I Am" statements: I am the gate and I am the good shepherd (John 10:7, 11). Jesus's "I Am" statements declared his divinity just as God had done with Moses on the mountain when he answered, "I AM WHO I AM" (Exod 3:14). The two predicate nouns "gate" and "shepherd" symbolized God's protection and provision. His kingdom reign differed from that of the human rule of their harsh Roman conquerors and the Jewish experts of the law who burdened the people with loads they could not carry (Luke 11:46). Jesus was the genuine shepherd who spent a great deal of time with his flock and knew each one. He led, cared for, and protected those who believed in him. They were his flock.

Jesus said, "I tell you the truth, I am the gate for the sheep" (John 10:7). In ancient Israel, shepherds built makeshift pens at night and slept at the opening to keep sheep from straying and to prevent predators from destroying the flock. Shepherds were literally the gate—sheep and predators would have to go through or

Appendix A

over them. In the morning, shepherds stood up, called the sheep by name, and led them to pasture.

Jesus also said, "I am the good shepherd. The good shepherd lays down his life for his sheep" (10:11). In biblical days, genuine shepherds protected and defended their sheep from predators. As a shepherd-boy, David fought bears and lions while guarding his sheep (1 Sam 17:34). Jesus Christ, our Good Shepherd, died a physical death for his sheep. He humbled himself on the cross and was obedient to death (Phil 2:8). His humility is associated with meekness or gentleness, which biblically is restrained power and disciplined strength. It is the gentleness of the strong. Jesus, the Lamb of God, gave up his life and took it up again in order to bring salvation to the world. Jesus expects Christian leaders to reflect his humble, meek strength and to cultivate Christian virtues, the sum of which is love. Christ's servant leaders are to reflect these attributes while serving as gatekeepers and good shepherds of their flock.

CHRISTIAN SHEPHERD-LEADERSHIP

Gatekeepers

Small group leaders function as gatekeepers when they advocate for what is okay and not okay to say and do in the group. They guard the group from those behaviors that inhibit member participation and disrupt the flow of conversation among members. Examples of disruptive behaviors are dominating members, the devil's advocate, silent members, and subgroups that exclude other members. If allowed to continue, such things adversely affect group cohesion and trust.

Dominating Members

People dominate groups in a variety of ways: they consistently tell long stories, routinely describe desperate situations, and/or give advice or comment after each person speaks. When diagramed, the group resembles a wheel with spokes pointing to a hub (the dominating member). Members do not talk to one another and cohesion dramatically drops. People tend to detach from groups where one person does most of the talking. For this reason, leaders should not dominate their group but they should encourage members to interact with one another.

The leader as gatekeeper changes the dynamic of a dominating member by establishing the expectation that each member be given the opportunity to talk. The leader might also need to deal directly with the dominating members. Below are several suggestions for dealing with the dominating member in a group situation:

"You have given us a lot to think about. Now let's hear from others."

"Everyone should be given a chance to speak." The leader smiles warmly, looks around the group, and continues, "Would someone comment on what's been said."

"You've made several good points. Now, we need to hear from others." The leader could then call on someone who has nonverbally signaled they have something to say.

Devil's Advocate

Some people control a group by habitually being the skeptic, prosecutor, chief debater, or provocateur. If left unchecked, only skilled debaters and confrontational people will participate in the group. Such a climate discourages trust, openness, vulnerability, and the exploration of new ideas. Gatekeepers protect the members by reading Scripture, setting limits, and/or talking privately with the person. The leader might say one of the following:

"Let's hear other opinions on this topic."

"You seem to be making the case that we should not believe in anything. Surely, this isn't what you intend. The Bible teaches that we are to be as shrewd as snakes and innocent as doves (Mark 10:16). We are to remain open to the Spirit of God and his Word but not be naïve to the very real presence of evil and human error. Let's return to our lesson."

"We know what you don't believe. Tell us what you do believe on this topic."

Appendix A

Silent Members

Quiet members tend to privately process information. They might be naturally shy or reluctant to talk in front of a group for other reasons. Whatever the reasons, their silence can make others feel uncomfortable. The leader might sit next to quieter members and occasionally ask them a question. Give them time to respond. The leader might converse with them before the meeting as people socialize. Quieter members might help in other ways, such as calling members when the study is cancelled, setting up for the meeting, or cleaning up after the group.

Subgroups

The formation of subgroups is a natural phenomenon in groups. People attend with a friend or spouse, or they have a natural affinity for one or two people within the group. Subgroups are a problem when they exclude other group members. The in-group/out-group dynamic fosters suspicion and mistrust. The leader should reach out to excluded members and mix up configurations through structured exercises. For example, leaders can occasionally ask members to discuss topics in pairs or threesomes and link people who don't normally talk with each other. After a designated period of time, the subgroups report back to the group.

Good Shepherds

Shepherd leaders perform nurturing and task functions for the group. They nurture as they attend to the social, emotional, and spiritual needs of members. They carry out task functions when they assume responsibility for the logistics of the meeting and completing the lessons. Both the nurturing and task functions contribute to the overall success of a group.

Appendix A

Nurturing Members:

1. Respond when people speak or non-verbally communicate. The leader might say, "Great, excellent comment." They encourage members by asking, "Can you say more about that?"
2. Extend grace to members and give people the benefit of the doubt.
3. Share your opinions or stories in a genuine, authentic manner.
4. Listen carefully to what people say and ask for clarification when appropriate.
5. Encourage members to draw close to God by example and through prayer.

Completing the Task:

1. Prepare well for each lesson.
2. Begin and end at the agreed-upon time. For example, meet at 6:30 p.m. for snacks and conversation, begin the meeting promptly at 7:00 p.m., and end at 8:30 p.m.
3. Keep the focus on the lesson and allow enough time for application and closing prayer.
4. When answering questions in the study guide, try to build on comments of other members.
5. Periodically summarize what's been said.
6. Read from the Bible at each meeting.
7. Emphasize Christ's victory over darkness.

A group goes through stages of development and in some sense has a life of its own. The group has a beginning, middle, and end; leadership styles change as the group moves though the stages. In the beginning, leaders are directive. Members are introduced to the topic of the lesson, to one another, and to the group format. As they develop familiarity with the subject, each other, and the

Appendix A

format, members become more spontaneous, involved, and productive. Though you remain the designated leader, members perform leadership functions. The leader becomes a facilitator and guide. As the group nears its end, members tend to detach, and the cohesion or glue of the group weakens. The leader becomes more directive as he or she guides the group to terminate the topic and group. You can choose one or more of the following questions when ending your group.

1. What has been most helpful to you in our study? Least helpful?
2. What are you taking away from our study that you can apply in everyday life?
3. Has your trust in God deepened as a result of our study? Are you more knowledgeable about the demonic realm?
4. What do you intend to do differently as a result of our study?
5. Can you suggest ways that we might improve on how we conducted our meetings?

Finally, conclude your group by praising God with songs or prayers. Pray for each other's needs and intercede for the Church, the lost, and the spiritually oppressed.

www.ingramcontent.com/pod-product-compliance
Lightning Source LLC
LaVergne TN
LVHW021619080426
835510LV00019B/2659